ADVENT and CHRISTMAS WISDOM
——— from ———
HENRI J.M. NOUWEN

Daily Scripture and Prayers
Together With Nouwen's Own Words

A Redemptorist Pastoral Publication

Liguori
LIGUORI, MISSOURI

Imprimi Potest:
Richard Thibodeau, C.Ss.R.
Provincial, Denver Province
The Redemptorists

Published by Liguori Publications
Liguori, Missouri
www.liguori.org

Library of Congress Cataloging-in-Publication Data

Nouwen, Henri J. M.
    Advent and Christmas wisdom from Henri J. M. Nouwen : daily Scripture and prayers together with Nouwen's own words.—1st ed.
        p. cm.—(A Redemptorist pastoral publication)
    ISBN 978-0-7648-0-1218-7
    1. Advent—Prayer-books and devotions—English. 2. Christmas—Prayer-books and devotions—English. 3. Catholic Church—Prayer-books and devotions—English. I. Title. II. Series.

BX2170.A4N68 2004
242'.33—dc22   2004048645

Acknowledgments of sources of quotations from Henri J. M. Nouwen are listed on pages 84–87.

Printed in the United States of America
17 16 15 14 13 / 11 10 9 8 7

Contents

Epigraph

THE ADVENT JOURNEY is an invitation to climb the mountain of the Lord. The journey consists of a slow, gradual ascending up the mountain path. As with all uphill climbing, there are certain dangers along the way, but also the joyful expectation of one day reaching the mountaintop that is the house of the Lord.

BROTHER VICTOR ANTOINE D'AVILA-LATOURRETTE

Introduction

HENRI J. M. NOUWEN (1932–1996) was born in the Netherlands into a staunchly Catholic family. Henri, the oldest of four children, had two brothers and one sister. From an early age he expressed a desire to enter the priesthood. Henri was ordained a priest for the Diocese of Utrecht in 1957.

After ordination, Henri spent six years studying psychology at the University of Nijmegen and two more years in training at the Menninger Institute in Topeka, Kansas.

Henri taught at Notre Dame and Harvard. Always restless, he spent time living as a monk in the Trappist Monastery of the Genesee in upstate New York, did further study at the Ecumenical Institute at Collegeville, Minnesota, and also served as a visiting scholar at the North American College in Rome. He also took up a temporary ministry to South America where he lived in Peru.

Returning to the United States, Henri taught briefly at Harvard and, upon meeting Jean Vanier, founder of L'Arche, an international group of communities that care for people with disabilities, accepted an invitation to become pastor for the L'Arche community of Daybreak in Toronto, Canada.

Henri took two sabbaticals from his work at Daybreak, one to recover from a severe depression, and the other to pursue his writing. Several weeks after his last sabbatical, Henri suffered two heart attacks.

As a priest, friend, author, lecturer, and counselor, Henri

was a popular figure. Among his books are *Intimacy: Pastoral Psychological Essays* (1969), *The Wounded Healer: Ministry in Contemporary Society* (1972), *Out of Solitude: Three Meditations on the Christian Life* (1974), *Clowning in Rome: Reflections on Solitude, Celibacy, Prayer, and Contemplation* (1979), *Making All Things New: An Invitation to the Spiritual Life* (1981), *Gracias! A Latin American Journal* (1983) along with many others.

How to Use This Book

ADVENT—that period of great anticipatory joy—is a time of preparation for the celebration of Christ's arrival in Bethlehem as a helpless infant. In the Western liturgy, Advent begins four Sundays prior to December 25—the Sunday closest to November 30 which is the feast of Saint Andrew, one of Jesus' first disciples.

The annual commemoration of Christ's birth begins the Christmas cycle of the liturgical year—a cycle which runs from Christmas Eve to the Sunday after the feast of the Epiphany. In keeping with the unfolding of the message of the liturgical year, this book is designed to be used during the entire period from the First Sunday of Advent to the end of the Christmas cycle.

The four weeks of Advent are often thought of as symbolizing the four different ways that Christ comes into the world: (1) at his birth as a helpless infant in Bethlehem; (2) at his arrival in the hearts of believers; (3) at his death; and (4) at his arrival on Judgment Day.

Because Christmas falls on a different day of the week each year, the fourth week of Advent is never really finished; it is abruptly, joyously, and solemnly abrogated by the annual coming again of Christ at Christmas. Christ's Second Coming will also one day abruptly interrupt our sojourn here on earth.

Since the calendar dictates the number of days in Advent, this book includes Scripture quotations and meditative excerpts from the works of Henri J. M. Nouwen for a full twenty-eight days. These twenty-eight daily readings make up Part I of the book. It is suggested that the reader begin at the beginning and, on Christmas Day, switch to Part II which contains materials for the twelve days of Christmas. If there are any "extra" entries from Part I, these may be read by doubling up days, if so desired, or by reading two entries on the weekends. Alternately, one may just skip those entries that do not fit within the Advent time frame for that particular year.

Each "day" in this book begins with the words of Henri Nouwen, taken from various sources which are acknowledged on pages 84 to 87. Following that quotation is an excerpt from Scripture, which is related in some way to the beginning quote. Next is provided a small prayer, also built on the ideas from the two preceding passages. Finally, an Advent or Christmas activity is suggested as a way to apply the messages to one's daily life.

PART I

~~~~~~~

READINGS *for* ADVENT

DAY 1

In the Midst of Our Dark World

*J*keep expecting loud and impressive events to convince me and others of God's saving power....Our temptation is to be distracted by them....When I have no eyes for the small signs of God's presence—the smile of a baby, the carefree play of children, the words of encouragement and gestures of love offered by friends—I will always remain tempted to despair.

The small child of Bethlehem, the unknown man of Nazareth, the rejected preacher, the naked man on the cross, *he* asks for my full attention. The work of our salvation takes place in the midst of a world that continues to shout, scream, and overwhelm us with its claims and promises.

HENRI J. M. NOUWEN,
GRACIAS! A LATIN AMERICAN JOURNAL

HIDDEN HOPE

A shoot shall come out from the
stump of Jesse.
and a branch shall grow out of
his roots.
The spirit of the LORD shall rest on him,
the spirit of wisdom and
understanding,
the spirit of counsel and might,
the spirit of knowledge and the
fear of the LORD.
His delight shall be in the fear of
the LORD.

ISAIAH 11:1–3

PRAYER

We welcome you, small child of Bethlehem, whose coming we await with quiet attention. Shield us from the
shouts, the screams, the empty promises of the season,
and encourage us to turn our hopes to your coming. We
know that the promise is hidden in the stable in Bethlehem and rooted in the offspring of Jesse; let us look for
our salvation there. Amen.

ADVENT ACTION

Today I will look for one small sign that God is present
in my daily life. I will give thanks for his presence. If he
is absent, I will resolve to find out why.

DAY 2

The Root of Patience

he French author Simone Weil writes in her notebook: "Waiting patiently in expectation is the foundation of the spiritual life." Without patience our expectation degenerates into wishful thinking. Patience comes from the word *"patior"* which means "to suffer."...What seems a hindrance becomes a way; what seems an obstacle becomes a door; what seems a misfit becomes a cornerstone.

HENRI J. M. NOUWEN, *OUT OF SOLITUDE*

BLESSINGS FALLING ON THE FAITHFUL

We are confident of better things. ....For God is not unjust; he will not overlook your work and the love that you showed for his sake in serving the saints, as you still do. And we want each one of you to show the same diligence so as to realize the full assurance of hope to the very end, so that you may not become sluggish, but imitators of those who through faith and patience inherit the promises.

HEBREWS 6:9–12

PRAYER

Lord, give us patience so that we may truly see obstacles as doors, the "not-quite-rights" of life as a foundation, our sufferings and indifference as eventual gateways to good works, to diligent service, and to our inheritance of salvation. Make the challenges on our spiritual journey into opportunities to say "yes" to your love. Amen.

ADVENT ACTION

Advent is marked by a spirit of expectation, by watchful alertness. Prepare the way of the Lord by making an Advent calendar of proposed contributions of service to others or positive changes in your own spiritual life. Don't plan too precisely, however; leave room for God's input.

DAY 3

In Solitude, In Activity

*S*omewhere we know that without a lonely place our lives are in danger. Somewhere we know that without silence words lose their meaning, that without listening speaking no longer heals, without distance closeness cannot cure. Somewhere we know that without a lonely place our actions quickly become empty gestures. The careful balance between silence and words, withdrawal and involvement, distance and closeness, solitude and community forms the basis of the Christian life and should therefore be the subjects of our most personal attention. Let us therefore look somewhat closer, first at our life in action, and at our life in solitude.

HENRI J. M. NOUWEN, *OUT OF SOLITUDE*

Preaching and Praying

In the morning, while it was still very dark, he got up and went out to a deserted place, and there he prayed. And Simon and his companions hunted for him. When they found him, they said to him, "Everyone is searching for you." He answered, "Let us go on to the neighboring towns, so that I may proclaim the message there also; for that is what I came out to do." And he went throughout Galilee, proclaiming the message in their synagogues and casting out demons.

MARK 1:35–39

Prayer

Lord, grant me a taste for solitude so that I might find in my heart the holy place where you live and can tell you truthfully how I am feeling. Grant me also an understanding of when to act in response to your call to me. Amen.

Advent Action

Our Lord went out to a deserted place to pray before he started his journey throughout Galilee to proclaim the message of the Good News. Look back on your past life and identify its active moments. Also examine the times of solitude you have experienced. Assess how you functioned under both conditions. Make sure that in the coming Advent season there is a balance between the two aspects of your spiritual journey.

DAY 4

How Do You Pray?

*T*ake the gospel of each day and spend ten minutes with it. Read it, and read it again. Walk into the world with the gospel in your heart. The gospel word of the day can become like a painting on the walls of your inner room, the inner room that is your heart….You have chances every second to live this Word, but it has to be in you. It can't be just an idea, it has to sink from the mind into the heart. That's prayer—to let God's Word speak deep within you and tell you, "You are my beloved."

HENRI J. M. NOUWEN INTERVIEW,
LIGUORIAN MAGAZINE, OCTOBER 1992

First Things First

"I tell you, do not worry about your life, what you will eat or what you will drink, or about your body, what you will wear. Is not life more than food, and the body more than clothing?...It is the Gentiles who strive for all these things; and indeed your heavenly Father knows that you need all these things. But strive first for the kingdom of God and his righteousness, and all these things will be given to you as well.

MATTHEW 6:25, 32–33

Prayer

Lord, I live "out in the open" for most of my everyday life. Let me find the offspring of the root of Jesse so that his grace and blessings will flow to my "outer life" where I must face the turmoil and temptations of life. Grant me also a recognition of the fact that my "inner life" with you is the greatest reality. Amen.

Advent Action

Find a scriptural motto to add to your Advent preparation calendar. Hold these words in your heart each day. Some suggestions might be as follows: "The Lord GOD will wipe away the tears from all faces" (Isa 25:8); "Should I not be concerned about Nineveh, that great city, in which there are more than a hundred and twenty thousand persons who do not know their right hand from their left?" (Jonah 9:11) or "Do not let loyalty and faithfulness forsake you; / bind them around your neck, / write them on the tablet of your heart" (Prov 3:3).

Staying Close to God

*I*f you want to follow Jesus…[you must] control what you take in every day. When you are on the bus or subway, or in your car, why busy your mind with all the garbage of advertisements? Why fill your mind with television and radio? Somehow you have to decide what your mind will receive. I don't mean you shouldn't ever go to movies or watch television, but control what enters your mind and heart. It's not just a question of pushing bad things out but a question of holding on to something really good.

It is good to have a prayer on your lips wherever you go. There are so many moments in life when you are free to pray. When you are waiting for the cashier in the supermarket, getting mad because he or she doesn't hurry, say a little prayer: "Lord, Jesus Christ, have mercy on me." Take that prayer with you wherever you go.

HENRI J. M. NOUWEN INTERVIEW,
LIGUORIAN MAGAZINE, OCTOBER 1992

PRAY ALWAYS

Be at peace among yourselves. And…admonish the idlers, encourage the fainthearted, help the weak, be patient with all of them. See that none of you repays evil for evil, but always seek to do good to one another and to all. Rejoice always, pray without ceasing, give thanks in all circum- -stances; for this is the will of God in Christ Jesus for you.

1 THESSALONIANS 5:12–18

PRAYER

Lord, let my life be an unceasing prayer to you despite its labors and losses; grant me a gracious heart that over- flows with a gratitude to overcome and wash away all my worries. Amen.

ADVENT ACTION

This Advent, be generous in your prayers for others and their well-being.

DAY 6

The Discipline of Community

*J*esus didn't live alone. He had Peter, John, and James around him. There were the Twelve and the other disciples. They formed circles of intimacy around Jesus. We too need these circles of intimacy, but it's a discipline. I choose L'Arche; L'Arche chooses me. I would be dead if I weren't here. I need people to love me and care for me.

Where are you getting your affection? Who's touching you? Who's holding you? Who makes you feel alive? Who says, "You are a beautiful person, you are the beloved of God, don't forget it"?

HENRI J. M. NOUWEN INTERVIEW,
LIGUORIAN MAGAZINE, OCTOBER 1992

A NEW LIFE

I...beg you to lead a life worthy of the calling to which you have been called, with all humility and gentleness, with patience, bearing with one another in love, making every effort to maintain the unity of the Spirit in the bond of peace. There is one body and one Spirit, just as you were called to the one hope of your calling, one Lord, one faith, one baptism, one God and Father of us all.

EPHESIANS 4:1–6

PRAYER

Lord, we ask for the discipline needed to be a true member of our communities. May we choose and be chosen to be God's beloved. Amen.

ADVENT ACTION

It is said that the original Christmas tree grew out of an evergreen that was part of the setting for the Medieval morality plays acted out on the steps of churches. This tree was used to represent the Garden of Eden. Create a small tree on which you hang apples (or their representation) to remind you of the failings that you wish to avoid this Advent. The apples, of course, stand for the fruit of the tree of good and evil with which Satan tempted Eve and Adam.

DAY 7

The Seeds of the False Self

The two main enemies of the spiritual life [are] anger and greed. They are the inner side of a secular life, the sour fruits of our worldly dependencies. What else is anger than the impulsive response to the experience of being deprived? When my sense of self depends on what others say of me, anger is a quite natural reaction to a critical word. And when my sense of self depends on what I can acquire, greed flares up when my desires are frustrated. Thus greed and anger are the brother and sister of a false self fabricated by the social compulsions of an unredeemed world....

It is not so strange that Anthony (d. 356 A.D., Father of Western Monasticism) and his fellow monks considered it a spiritual disaster to accept passively the tenets and values of their society. They had come to appreciate how hard it is not only for the individual Christian but also for the Church itself to escape the seductive compulsions of the world.

HENRI J. M. NOUWEN,
THE WAY OF THE HEART

TRANSFORMATION IN CHRIST

Present your bodies as a living sacrifice, holy and acceptable to God, which is your spiritual worship. Do not be conformed to the world, but be transformed by the renewing of your minds, so that you may discern what is the will of God—what is good and acceptable and perfect.

ROMANS 12:1–2

PRAYER

Lord, renew our souls so that we may find what is good and acceptable and perfect in your eyes. Open our eyes to see beyond the lures of the world—the prizes of success, the rewards of wealth and position, the seductions of a modern life lived out at a frenetic and competitive pace. Help us to sever our dependencies on the world's distractions and give us an opportunity to find ourselves in the shelter and safety of your wings. Amen.

ADVENT ACTION

Forego one of the world's distractions for a day: television, all-but-the-necessary phone calls, negative comments about anyone, music in the car on the way to work, busy work of any kind, surfing the Internet, reading magazines, or so on.

Compassion Demands Solidarity

f you would ask the Desert Fathers why solitude gives birth to compassion, they would say, "Because it makes us die to our neighbor." At first this answer seems quite disturbing to a modern mind. But when we give it a closer look we can see that in order to be of service to others we have to die to them; that is, we have to give up measuring our meaning and value with the yardstick of others. To die to our neighbors means to stop judging them, to stop evaluating them, and thus to become free to be compassionate. Compassion can never coexist with judgment because judgment creates the distance, the distinction, which prevents us from really being with the other.

HENRI J. M. NOUWEN,
THE WAY OF THE HEART

JUDGING OTHERS

"Do not judge, and you will not be judged; do not condemn, and you will not be condemned, Forgive, and you will be forgiven, give, and it will be given to you. A good measure, pressed down, shaken together, running over, will be put into your lap; for the measure you give will be the measure you get back."

LUKE 6:37–38

PRAYER

Lord, endow us with discernment so that we might recognize the seeds of harshness in our lives. Help us to overcome this harshness with the heart of compassion, seeing then your presence in all human beings. Amen.

ADVENT ACTION

A follower of Saint Anthony, Abba Moses, gives this instruction: "Do not let dislike dominate your heart." Make a short list of those whom you dislike, even surreptitiously. Choose one person to expunge from your negative thoughts.

DAY 9

Mary, Our Mother

*M*ary creates a space for us where we can become children as Jesus became a child….It is precisely this childhood that Mary wants us to claim. She who offered an immaculate space for God to take on human flesh wants to offer us a space where we can be reborn as Jesus was born. With the same heart that loved Jesus, she wants to love us. It is a heart that will not make us wonder anxiously whether we are truly loved. It is a heart that has not been marked by the infidelities of the human race and so will never bring wounds to those who seek peace there.

HENRI J. M. NOUWEN, *JESUS & MARY:*
FINDING OUR SACRED CENTER

CHILDREN OF GOD

See what love the Father has given us, that we should be called children of God; and that is what we are. The reason the world does not know us is that it did not know him. Beloved, we are God's children now; what we will be has not yet been revealed.

1 JOHN 3:1–2

PRAYER

Lord, your mother, Mary, and her "yes" to God's request is central to the Advent mystery. Help us to become her children and yours, so we may be enveloped in the confidence of being truly loved and cared for by you both. Make it possible for us to say our "yes" to your invitations, no matter how reluctantly we may do so. Amen.

ADVENT ACTION

Place flowers in front of our Lady's statue or picture in honor of her major role in our salvation story. If you wish to celebrate a bit differently, follow a custom that is observed in Sicily where it is customary to bake the season's first *sfinciuni*, a type of pizza made with simple ingredients: flour, yeast, onions, anchovies, olive oil, and crumbs of leftover bread. Though probably not available in many places in the U.S., have a pizza of your choice *"per la Madonna."*

DAY 10

Passionate Waiting

*I*f it is true that God in Jesus Christ is waiting for our response to divine love, then we can discover a whole new perspective on how to wait in life. We can learn to be obedient people who do not always try to go back to the action but who recognize the fulfillment of our deepest humanity in passion, in waiting. If we can do this, I am convinced that we will come in touch with the glory of God and our own new life.

HENRI J. M. NOUWEN,
"THE SPIRITUALITY OF WAITING," *WEAVINGS*, JANUARY 1987

WAITING FOR THE LORD

On this mountain the LORD of hosts
will make for all peoples
a feast of rich food, a feast of
well-aged wines....
Then the Lord GOD will wipe away
the tears from all faces,
and the disgrace of his people he
will take away from all the earth,
for the LORD has spoken.
It will be said on that day,
Lo, this is our God; we have
waited for him, so that he might save us.
This is the LORD for whom we have waited;
let us be glad and rejoice in his salvation.

ISAIAH 25:6, 8–9

PRAYER

Lord, our Saving Light who came to set us free, shine upon us in your glory. May your light provide illumination for us so that we recognize all those who need our help, however much, however little. Keep us from straying into the works of darkness, wipe away our tears, and grant us your light and blessings. Amen.

ADVENT ACTION

Obedience to God's plan for us should really be unqualified. For today, give a "yes, always" instead of a "yes, but" to God's requests; the word "but" inserts a condition into our relationship with God and signifies less than wholehearted acceptance.

Claiming True Peace

Keep your eyes on the prince of peace, the one who doesn't cling to his divine power; the one who refuses to turn stones into bread, jump from great heights, and rule with great power...; the one who touches the lame, the crippled, and the blind, the one who speaks words of forgiveness and encouragement....Keep your eyes on him who becomes poor with the poor, weak with the weak. He is the source of all peace.

HENRI J. M. NOUWEN,
"ADAM'S STORY," *WEAVINGS*, MARCH–APRIL, 1988.

BLESSINGS ABOUND

Clothe yourselves with compassion, kindness, humility, meekness, and patience. Bear with one another and, if anyone has a complaint against another, forgive each other; just as the Lord has forgiven you, so you also must forgive. Above all, clothe yourselves with love, which binds everything together in perfect harmony. And let the peace of Christ rule in your hearts.

COLOSSIANS 3:12–15

PRAYER

Lord, help us to make our way to Bethlehem, to the peace of the Christ Child that withstood even the humility of his birth in a stable. Let us seek harmony in our lives as the angels did when they announced the Christ Child's birth in perfect praise. Amen.

ADVENT ACTION

Liturgical music can often help us pray and can even help to overcome the chaos of a tense situation at home or elsewhere. Though the air waves are inundated with "Christmas" music immediately after Thanksgiving, instead find and listen to a CD or tape of religious music that expresses the calm serenity of waiting for the Christ Child: Gregorian chant, Bach's *Advent Cantatas*, or liturgical music recorded by various choirs might be good choices.

DAY 12

Walking in the Presence of God

We must continually remind ourselves that the first commandment requiring us to love God with all our heart, all our soul, and all our mind is indeed the first. I wonder if we really believe this. It seems that in fact we live as if we should give as much of our heart, soul, and mind as possible to our fellow human beings, while trying hard not to forget God....But Jesus' claim is much more radical. He asks for a single-minded commitment to God and God alone. God wants all of our heart, all of our mind, and all of our soul.

HENRI J. M. NOUWEN,
THE LIVING REMINDER

LOVE IS ALL

When the Pharisees heard that he [Jesus] had silenced the Sadducees, they gathered together, and one of them, a lawyer, asked him a question to test him. "Teacher, which command-ment in the law is the greatest?" He said to him, "'You shall love the Lord your God with all your heart, and with all your soul, and with all your mind.' This is the greatest and first commandment."

MATTHEW 22:34–38

PRAYER

Lord, you have revealed your love to me by coming into this world as a helpless child, human in all except sin. Let me respond to this great gift of love by making your love a reality in this world. Keep me rooted in your love and let me flower into a new person transformed by the giving and receiving of your grace. Amen.

ADVENT ACTION

Often we remain so mired in the perceived sadness of the "old tapes" running through our heads that we cannot acknowledge God's love for us. Pick one "old tape": a resentment, a belittlement, a loss, and pack it away permanently in exchange for the shelter of a loved and loving God.

DAY 13

Real Listening

The word "listening" in Latin is *obedire*, and *audire* means "listening with great attention." That is where the word "obedience" comes from. Jesus is called the obedient one, that means the listener. The Latin word for not listening, being deaf, is "*surdus.*" If you are absolutely not listening, that is where the word "absurd" comes from. So it might be interesting to note that somebody who is not listening is leading an absurd life....

Now, to become a listener, one way to do it is to say, "How can I let the 'Lord is my Shepherd, there is nothing I shall want,'" enter in from my mind to my heart? I can say it is here and that is just a statement, but it becomes prayer when I experience the shepherding presence of God in the center of my being....Listening starts precisely when you move from the mind to the heart and let the truth of your being center you down.

HENRI J. M. NOUWEN, "DISCOVERING OUR GIFT THROUGH SERVICE
TO OTHERS," SPEECH GIVEN TO MEMBERS OF FADICA, 1994

A Good Shepherd

The LORD is my shepherd, I shall not want.
He makes me lie down in green pastures;...
He leads me in right paths
  for his name's sake.

Even though I walk through the darkest valley,
  I fear no evil;
for you are with me;
  your rod and your staff—
  they comfort me....

Surely goodness and mercy shall follow me
  all the days of my life,
and I shall dwell in the house of the LORD
  my whole life long.
                                    PSALM 23:1–4, 6

Prayer

Lord, help us to rein in all the distractions that bombard us daily. Let us pay our full attention to you. Let us truly listen to your requests. Keep us from the shortsighted absurdity of bestowing our attention on the wrong things. Amen.

Advent Action

A prisoner of war spent part of his captivity in an effort to remember all the words of the Twenty-Third Psalm. Often, in profoundly difficult situations, we are at a loss for words to pray. Memorize a prayer that you feel will be helpful to you in times of trouble.

The Sacred Encounter

I am deeply moved by the simple and mysterious encounter [of the Visitation]....Two women meet each other and affirm in each other the promise given to them. The humanly impossible has happened to them. God has come to them to begin the salvation promised through the ages. Through these two women God has decided to change the course of history. Who could ever understand? Who could ever believe it? Who could ever let it happen....For three months Mary and Elizabeth live together and encourage each other to truly accept the motherhood given to them. Mary's presence makes Elizabeth more fully aware of becoming the mother of the "prophet of the Most High" (Lk 1:76), and Elizabeth's presence allows Mary to grow in the knowledge of becoming the Mother of the "Son of the Most High" (Lk 1:32).

The story of the Visitation teaches me the meaning of friendship and community. How can I ever let God's grace fully work in my life unless I live in a community of people who can affirm it, deepen it, and strengthen it?

HENRI J. M. NOUWEN,
THE ROAD TO DAYBREAK

COMING TOGETHER IN GOD'S GRACE

In those days [after the Annunciation] Mary set out and went with haste to a Judean town in the hill country, where she entered the house of Zechariah and greeted Elizabeth. When Elizabeth heard Mary's greeting, the child [John the Baptist] leaped in her womb. And Elizabeth was filled with the Holy Spirit and exclaimed with a loud cry, "Blessed are you among women, and blessed is the fruit of your womb." ...And Mary remained with her about three months and then returned to her home.

LUKE 1:39–41, 56

PRAYER

Lord, as we prepare for your birth as Mary's Son, may we find our own "Elizabeth" to be a refuge of wisdom, comfort, and joy. Let us acknowledge to you that we are never too old, never too filled with the effects of sin, never too far away to receive you and your Mother with all hospitality and trust. Amen.

ADVENT ACTION

Commemorate Mary of the Visitation, Handmaid of the Lord, by offering gentle assistance to someone in your environment who is in need: of praise, of a good word, of day-brightening laughter.

DAY 15

The Coming of the Lord

℩t is Advent again. In his sermon this morning, Oscar Uzin said: "Be alert, be alert, so that you will be able to recognize your Lord in your husband, your wife, your parents, your children, your friends, your teachers, but also in all that you read in the daily papers. The Lord is coming, always coming. Be alert to his coming. When you have ears to hear and eyes to see, you will recognize him at any moment of your life. Life is Advent; life is recognizing the coming of the Lord.

HENRI J. M. NOUWEN,
GRACIAS! A LATIN AMERICAN JOURNAL

Keep Awake and Watch

"But about that day or hour no one knows, neither the angels in heaven, nor the Son, but only the Father. Beware, keep alert; for you do not know when the time will come. It is like a man going on a journey, when he leaves home and puts his slaves in charge, each with his work, and commands the doorkeeper to be on the watch. Therefore, keep awake—for you do not know when the master of the house will come, in the evening, or at midnight, or at cockcrow, or at dawn, or else he may find you asleep when he comes suddenly."

MARK 13:32–36

Prayer

Lord Emmanuel, Prince of Peace, let us be especially alert to your coming during this Advent. As a parent listens for the cry of an infant, as a sailor watches for land, as an astronomer scans the skies, as a doctor watches for signs of returning health, let us be attentive to your arrival. Let not our pride and arrogance blind us and put us to sleep. Give us the endurance to be true watchers of the night as we journey through this Advent. Amen.

Advent Action

We are in a state of readiness when we wait in wisdom like the wise virgins of the parable. Get up fifteen minutes early or retire fifteen minutes later in order to devote time to watchful waiting and prayer.

DAY 16

Divine Heart of Love

The Father's love was so unlimited that he wanted us to know that love and to find in it the fulfillment of our deepest desires. So, he sent us you, dear Lord Jesus, with a human heart big enough to hold all human loneliness and all human anguish. Your heart is not a heart of stone but a heart of flesh; your heart of flesh is not narrowed by human sin and unfaithfulness, but is as wide and deep as divine love itself. Your heart does not distinguish between rich and poor, friend and enemy, female and male, slave and free, sinner and saint. Your heart is open to receive anyone with total, unrestricted love.

HENRI J. M NOUWEN, *HEART SPEAKS TO HEART*

The Sacred Heart of Jesus

"Come to me, all you that are weary and are carrying heavy burdens, and I will give you rest. Take my yoke upon you, and learn from me; for I am gentle and humble in heart, and you will find rest for your souls. For my yoke is easy, and my burden is light."

MATTHEW 11:28–30

Prayer

Lord, let us place wreaths on the doors of our own hearts, so that the Holy Spirit may find these doors, enter in, and take up his lodging there, and by his presence, make us holy. We ask that the entrance of the Holy Spirit create an island of calm and gentleness within us. Amen.

Advent Action

Place a laurel wreath on a door or in a window in order to symbolize the victory over sin achieved by Christ's entry into our world.

DAY 17

Do You Love Me?

*A*t issue here is the question: "To whom do I belong? To God or to the world?"…As long as I keep running about asking "Do you love me? Do you really love me?" I give all power to the voices of the world and put myself in bondage because the world is filled with "ifs." The words says: "Yes, I love you *if* you are good-looking, intelligent, and wealthy. I love you *if* you have a good education, a good job, and good connections. I love you *if* you produce much, sell much, and buy much." There are endless "ifs" hidden in the world's love. These "ifs" enslave me, since it is impossible to respond adequately to all of them. The world's love is and always will be conditional. As long as I keep looking for my true self in the world of conditional love, I will remain "hooked" to the world—trying, failing, and trying again.

HENRI J. M. NOUWEN, *THE RETURN OF THE PRODIGAL SON: THE STORY OF HOMECOMING*

ONLY CHOOSE

I have set before you today life and prosperity, death and adversity. If you obey the commandments of the LORD your God that I am commanding you today, by loving the LORD your God, walking in his ways, and observing his command--ments, decrees, and ordinances, then you shall live and become numerous, and the LORD your God will bless you. ...But if your heart turns away and you do not hear, but are led astray to bow down to other gods and serve them, I declare to you today that you shall perish.

DEUTERONOMY 30:15–18

PRAYER

Lord, let the doubts hidden behind the question "Do you love me?" disappear as we advance through this Advent. Strengthen us to observe lovingly your commandments and precepts. Let openness to your love be the watchword of our hearts. Amen.

ADVENT ACTION

Spend the day in a conscious effort to comprehend the fact that you are God's beloved. Banish the "ifs," the conditions that bar our confidence in God's love.

DAY 18

Temptation to Power

One of the greatest ironies of the history of Christianity is that its leaders constantly gave in to the temptation of power —political power, military power, economic power, or moral and spiritual power—even though they continued to speak in the name of Jesus, who did not cling to his divine power but emptied himself and became as we are. The temptation to consider power an apt instrument for the proclamation of the Gospel is the greatest of all....With this rationalization, crusades took place; inquisitions were organized; Indians were enslaved; positions of great influence were desired. Every time we see a major crisis in the history of the Church...we always see that a major cause of rupture is the power exercised by those who claim to be followers of the poor and powerless Jesus.

What makes the temptation of power so seemingly irresistible? Maybe it is that power offers an easy substitute for the hard task of love. It seems easier to be God than to love God,

easier to control people than to love people, easier to own life
than to love life.

HENRI J. M. NOUWEN, *IN THE NAME OF JESUS*

IMITATE CHRIST'S HUMILITY

*Let each of you look not to your own interests, but to the interests
of others. Let the same mind be in you that was in Christ Jesus,*
who, though he was in the form of God,
did not regard equality with God
as something to be exploited,
but emptied himself,
taking the form of a slave,
being born in human likeness.
And being found in human form
he humbled himself
and became obedient to the point of death—
even death on a cross.

PHILIPPIANS 2:4–8

PRAYER

Lord, instruct us in the ways of humility so that we may
banish our unwarranted pride that keeps us from finding
you on this Advent journey. Help us to place our enslaving
need for control and power into your loving hands where
we will find our true freedom. Amen.

ADVENT ACTION

Today give up on the need to control others, whether it be
scheduling a meeting, expecting others to drive as you
wish, or making your preferences a priority over those
of others.

DAY 19

Prepare the Way of the Lord

*P*ère Thomas keeps telling us in his sermons that the days before Christmas must be days of deep prayer to prepare our hearts for the coming of Christ. We must be really ready to receive him. Christ wants to be born in us, but we must be open, willing, receptive, and truly welcoming. To become that way we have Advent and especially the last days before Christmas….

This morning I thought the day was completely free and open for prayer. Now it is evening, and I don't know where the time went. Somehow the externals of Christmas—presents, decorations, short visits—took over the day and drained away like water through a poorly built dike. How hard it is to remember…the difference between the urgent and the important!

HENRI J. M. NOUWEN, *THE ROAD TO DAYBREAK*

BORN AGAIN

Now that you have purified your souls by your obedience to the truth so that you have genuine mutual love, love one another deeply from the heart. You have been born anew, not of perishable but of imperishable seed, through the living and enduring word of God.

1 PETER 1:22–23

PRAYER

Lord, lead us out of the prison of our sin into the freedom of your saving love; lead us out of darkness into the light of your grace; lead us out of the shadow of death into the promise of eternal life. Amen.

ADVENT ACTION

Salt is a sign of purification in the New Testament. Give up salting your food today as acknowledgment of your new birth in Christ brought about by his coming.

DAY 20

True Identity

*J*esus' whole message is to say that you are God's beloved child....When you can hear in your heart, not in your head, that you are truly God's beloved daughter, that you are truly God's beloved son, everything turns around. The mystery of this spiritual truth is that you were loved before you were born, and you will be loved after you die....Your dwelling in God's heart is a dwelling from eternity to eternity.

HENRI J. M. NOUWEN,
"DISCOVERING OUR GIFT THROUGH SERVICE TO OTHERS,"
SPEECH GIVEN TO MEMBERS OF FADICA, 1994

Our Mission

Listen to me, O coastlands,
*   pay attention, you peoples from far away!*
The LORD called me before I was born,
*   while I was in my mother's womb he named me.*
He made my mouth like a sharp sword,
*   in the shadow of his hand he hid me.*

ISAIAH 49:1–2

Now the word of the LORD came to me saying:
"Before I formed you in the womb I knew you,
*   and before you were born I consecrated you;*
I appointed you a prophet to the nations."

JEREMIAH 1:4–5

Prayer

Lord, you who knew us before we were ever born, you who consecrated us into your care, hold us in the shadow of your hand and watch over us this Advent. Make its observance a shining path to our home and banquet with you in heaven. Amen.

Advent Action

Holly (or before the seventeen century, "holy tree") is strongly associated with the season of Advent and Christmas. Its bright red berries have been seen as symbolizing the joy of the Virgin at bearing the Christ Child, and also as a symbol of the drops of blood from the body of Jesus at Calvary. Wear a sprig of holly as a sign of our goal to do good and as a symbol of eternal life.

DAY 21

Belovedness Belongs to All

*Q*uite often out of an intimate encounter with God encounters with other human beings become possible....If you are the beloved of God, if you start thinking about other people's lives, you start realizing that they are as beloved as you are. One of the profound experiences of the spiritual life is that when you discover yourself as being the beloved son or daughter of God, you suddenly have new eyes to see the belovedness of other people.

It is very interesting because it is the opposite of what happens in the world when they say you are very special, that means you are not the same as the rest. If you win an award and they say you are different than others, then that award is valuable because not everybody gets that award. The world is saying that you are only the best when not everybody else is the best.

HENRI J. M. NOUWEN,
"DISCOVERING OUR GIFT THROUGH SERVICE TO OTHERS,"
SPEECH GIVEN TO MEMBERS OF FADICA, 1994

Who Is the Greatest?

Then they came to Capernaum; and when [Jesus] was in the house he asked [his disciples], "What were you arguing about on the way?" But they were silent, for on the way they had argued with one another who was the greatest. He sat down, called the twelve, and said to them, "Whoever wants to be first must be last of all and servant of all."

MARK 9:33–35

Prayer

Lord, take away our desires to be the best, the greatest, the first, the most famous, the most popular, the wealthiest, the most powerful. Instead, grant us a true spirit of repentance and a willingness to be the last, the least, the lowliest, the poorest, the smallest, the least important. Amen.

Advent Action

Make a list of the blessings and benefits that have been given to you by God, your Savior. Take a few minutes today to give thanks for one of these undeserved blessings. If possible, pass this blessing on to others.

DAY 22

Betrayal

*P*arker Palmer, a spiritual writer of the Quaker tradition, says community is the place where the person you least want to live with always lives. So community is not like a place where you love each other sort of freely and warmly and affectionately. Community is in fact the place where you are purified, where your love is tested, where your childhood of God is constantly put through the mill of human relationships. That is what community is. Community is a place where Judas always is and sometimes it is just you.

HENRI J. M. NOUWEN,
"DISCOVERING OUR GIFT THROUGH SERVICE TO OTHERS,"
SPEECH GIVEN TO MEMBERS OF FADICA, 1994

THE TWELVE

Then Jesus summoned his twelve disciples and gave them authority over unclean spirits, to cast them out, and to cure every disease and every sickness. These are the names of the twelve apostles: first, Simon, also known as Peter, and his brother Andrew; James son of Zebedee, and his brother John; Philip and Bartholomew; Thomas and Matthew the tax collector; James son of Alphaeus, and Thaddaeus; Simon the Cananaean, and Judas Iscariot, the one who betrayed him.

MATTHEW 10:1–4

PRAYER

Lord, help us to see our membership in community as a necessary way to pray and to proceed on our journey. Though, as a paraphrase of Robert Frost says, "Community is often a place where they have to take you in." Let us understand our gatherings into church, family, and neighborhood as a way to find you in the midst of imperfections and humanness—especially our own. Amen.

ADVENT ACTION

Though we cannot often escape our compulsions to afflict the world with our own unpleasant idiosyncracies, for today, love enough to remove one annoyance you know is a cause of irritation to another.

DAY 23

Being Forgiven

*I*n forgiving we are still in control, "I forgive you." But to be forgiven by you means first of all I have to say, "I'm sorry. There is something that I didn't do for you." That is hard and puts me in a vulnerable position, in a dependent position. I have handed you over to suffering....Somehow I have failed you. I am sorry I failed you. I am sorry that I wasn't the kind of mother, or father, or friend, or brother, or sister, or neighbor, whatever that I wanted to be. Can you forgive me? It is not just asking the individual. It is having the ability to say, "God, can you forgive me?" Can I be open to forgiveness? Then your heart can move from the hardened heart to a heart of flesh.

HENRI J. M. NOUWEN,
"DISCOVERING OUR GIFT THROUGH SERVICE TO OTHERS,"
SPEECH GIVEN TO MEMBERS OF FADICA, 1994

Forgive Us Our Sins

Be on your guard! If another disciple sins, you must rebuke the offender, and if there is repentance, you must forgive. And if the same person sins against you seven times a day, and turns back to you seven times and says, 'I repent,' you must forgive."

LUKE 17:3–4

Prayer

Lord of Mercy, you are in each and in all of us. Help us to understand and acknowledge that this is why we must forgive and ask forgiveness. Let us see your face shine out of the countenances of all peoples. Amen.

Advent Action

Ask forgiveness of one person today. Let each person you meet today leave your presence a happier person.

DAY 24

An Invitation

God came to us because he wanted to join us on the road, to listen to our story, and to help us realize that we are not walking in circles but moving towards the house of peace and joy. This is the great mystery of Christmas that continues to give us comfort and consolation: we are not alone on our journey. The God of love who gave us life sent us his only Son to be with us at all times and in all places, so that we never have to feel lost in our struggles but always can trust that he walks with us....

Christmas is the renewed invitation not to be afraid and let him—whose love is greater than our own hearts and minds can comprehend—be our companion.

HENRI J. M. NOUWEN,
GRACIAS! A LATIN AMERICAN JOURNAL

Worry Not

"Do not be afraid, little flock, for it is your Father's good pleasure to give you the kingdom. Sell your possessions and give alms. Make purses for yourselves that do not wear out, an unfailing treasure in heaven, where no thief comes near and no moth destroys."

LUKE 12:32–33

Prayer

Lord, give us the grace to be counted among your "little flock." You often said to your disciples, "Be not afraid." May your message sink into our hearts and offer us merciful consolation and joyful assurances of your unending care and concern. Amen.

Advent Action

Poet Robert Herrick says this about the mistletoe plant, a symbol of the Christmas season: "Lord, I am like to mistletoe, / Which has no root and cannot grow / Or prosper, but by that same tree / It clings about: so I by thee." Note that mistletoe is a parasite that often grows under the bark of apple trees. Include a sprig of mistletoe in your Christmas greens to signify undying love for our Lord and our unalloyed dependence on him. By the way, an old legend says that Christ's cross was made of the wood from mistletoe.

DAY 25

Christmas Touches the Whole of Creation

*S*omehow I realized that songs, music, good feelings, beautiful liturgies, nice presents, big dinners, and many sweet words do not make Christmas. Christmas is saying "yes" to something beyond all emotions and feelings. Christmas is saying "yes" to a hope based on God's initiative, which has nothing to do with what I think or feel. Christmas is believing that the salvation of the world is God's work and not mine. Things will never look just right or feel just right. If they did, someone would be lying.... But it is into this broken world that a child is born who is called Son of the Most High, Prince of Peace, Savior.

HENRI J. M. NOUWEN,
THE ROAD TO DAYBREAK

THE BIRTH OF JESUS

In those days a decree went out from Emperor Augustus
that all the world should be registered....All went to their
own towns to be registered. Joseph also went from the town
of Nazareth in Galilee to Judea, to the city of David called
Bethlehem, because he was descended from the house and
family of David. He went to be registered with Mary, to
whom he was engaged and who was expecting a child. While
they were there, the time came for her to deliver her child.
And she gave birth to her firstborn son and wrapped him
in bands of cloth, and laid him in a manger, because there
was no place for them in the inn.

LUKE 2:1–7

PRAYER

Lord, let us pray with Henri Nouwen, saying: "Thank
you, Lord, that you came independently of my feelings
and thoughts. Your heart is greater than mine." We welcome you. Amen.

ADVENT ACTION

Give at least one spiritual gift this season: a novena for a
loved one, a spiritual book, a Mass.

DAY 26

From Morals to Mysticism

Mysticism is for all, not just for a few special people. Based on our baptism, all are called to a mystical life, to communion with God. We need to claim that, to taste it, and feel it, to trust that the deeper we live this communion, the more our behavior will witness to the truth.

For many, religion has to do with what we are allowed to do and not allowed to do. In the end, that doesn't bear fruit. The great challenge is to discover that we are truly invited to participate in the divine life of the Father, the Son, and the Holy Spirit.

HENRI J. M. NOUWEN
INTERVIEW, *LIGUORIAN* MAGAZINE, OCTOBER 1992

WE ARE CALLED

His divine power has given us everything needed for life and godliness, through the knowledge of him who called us by his own glory and goodness. Thus he has given us, through these things, his precious and very great promises, so that through them you may escape from the corruption that is in the world because of lust, and may become participants of the divine nature.

2 PETER 1:3–4

PRAYER

Lord, draw yourself down into our hearts and let us grow in likeness to you until we find eternal love and salvation in your presence, here and hereafter. Amen.

ADVENT ACTION

Set up a personal reminder of the coming of our Lord. This might be a framed Scripture passage, a work of art, and an artifact from nature. Incorporate this symbol into your daily meditation environment.

DAY 27

A Sacred Center

I know that I am called to live at the place of innocence: the place where Jesus chose to live. There he made his home and asks me to make mine. In that place I am loved and well held. There I do not have to be afraid....Can I choose to make my innocence my home, think from there, speak from there, act from there?

I know that every time I choose for my innocence I don't have to worry about the next ten years. I can simply be where I am... always sure that I am not alone but with him who called me to live as God's child.

HENRI J. M. NOUWEN,
JESUS & MARY: FINDING OUR SACRED CENTER

Father, Protect Them in Your Name

I am not asking you to take them out of the world, but I ask you to protect them from the evil one. They do not belong to the world, just as I do not belong to the world. Sanctify them in the truth; your word is truth.

John 17:15–17

Prayer

Lord, affix us in a firm and sure spot where we are safe from the Herods of this world. During these days of rejoicing, keep us wrapped in the "swaddling clothes" of your embrace and safely in your lap of love. Amen.

Advent Action

Take a five-minute break to notice a single object in your environment and trace its origins. For example, a book may be made of paper imported from another country, with text on it edited by an employee of a company a thousand miles away, formatted by a graphic designer, its cover created by an artist and its content created by an author, and so on. Trace these components back to the ultimate Creator God and say a word of thanksgiving for his generosity.

Feliz Navidad!

*T*he joyful celebration [of Midnight Mass] unfolded with mystery and a few surprises, the first of which announced itself as a mechanical bird hidden in the Christmas tree! A large silver ball produced loud bird calls at regular intervals and the layman who acted as deacon during the liturgy was so enchanted with this gadget that he turned it on at the most unusual moments....

While celebrating the Eucharist, Peter and I were surrounded by baby dolls, small and large, naked and elaborately dressed....I never saw so many Jesus-babies together in my life. I soon found out that it belongs to the folk tradition that the baby Jesus has to hear Mass on Christmas day. Therefore families take their Christmas child out of his stable and bring him to church.

HENRI J. M. NOUWEN,
GRACIAS! A LATIN AMERICAN JOURNAL

INNOCENCE OF INFANTS

Like newborn infants, long for the pure, spiritual milk, so that by it you may grow into salvation—if indeed you have tasted that the Lord is good.

1 PETER 2:2–3

PRAYER

Lord, give us your spiritual milk, your bread and wine, your body and blood, that we may be sated and satisfied with the taste of salvation. Refurbish us as new Adams and new Eves. Amen.

ADVENT ACTION

Resolve to wait in patience today to see the Lord's hand in the celebration of his coming. Listen twice as much as you speak. Listen especially to the members of your family whose voices may have become all too familiar and therefore ignored.

PART II

~~~~~~~

Readings

for the

Christmas

Season

DAY 1

The Name of Jesus

The conviction that Francis Avenue, on which Harvard Divinity School stands, was named after St. Francis....I must have suppressed my inclination to verify this conviction out of fear of being robbed of another illusion....

Names tell stories, most of all the name which is above all other names, the name of Jesus. In his name I am called to live. His name has to become my house, my dwelling place, my refuge, my ark. His name has to start telling the story of being born, growing up, growing old, and dying—revealing a God who loved us so much that he sent his only child to us.

HENRI J. M. NOUWEN,
THE ROAD TO DAYBREAK

PERSECUTION IN JESUS' NAME

"I will give you words and a wisdom that none of your opponents will be able to withstand or contradict. You will be betrayed even by parents and brothers, by relatives and friends; and they will put some of you to death. You will be hated by all because of my name. But not a hair of your head will perish."

LUKE 21:15–18

PRAYER

Lord, though you have counted all the hairs of our heads (see Lk 12:7), though you have taken our well-being to your very heart, we still must withstand the betrayal of those around us as you withstood the betrayal of your disciple Judas Iscariot. Help us to endure this treachery, this hatred, in your name. Amen.

CHRISTMAS ACTION

Today remember to pray with the psalmist: "O LORD, how majestic is your name in all the earth!" (Ps 8:1).

DAY 2

Consolation

*T*here is a much more human option to reevaluate the past as a continuing challenge to surrender ourselves to an unknown future. It is the option to understand our experience of powerlessness as an experience of being guided, even when we do not know exactly where....We can see that a growing surrender to the unknown is a sign of spiritual maturity and does not take away autonomy. Death [of a loved one] is indeed an invitation to surrender ourselves more freely to the future, in the conviction that one of the most important parts of our lives may still be ahead of us.

HENRI J. M. NOUWEN, *A LETTER OF CONSOLATION*

The Cinch of Discipleship

"Very truly, I tell you, when you were younger, you used to fasten your own belt and to go wherever you wished. But when you grow old, you will stretch out your hands, and someone else will fasten a belt around you and take you where you do not wish to go."

JOHN 21:18

Prayer

Lord, wherever you lead, let us follow. Wherever we are taken, let us go willingly. Let us firmly believe that the paths you point out to us are the ones we must take. Let us be eagerly on the road with you. Amen.

Christmas Action

Today thank God for the giftedness and company of another.

Stretching Out Our Hearts to God

*I*t is not we who pray, but the Spirit of God who prays in us....When our heart belongs to God, the world and its powers cannot steal it from us. When God has become the Lord of our heart, our basic alienation is overcome....

When God has become our shepherd, our refuge, our fortress, when we can reach out to him in the midst of a broken world and feel at home while still on the way. When God swells in us, we can enter in a wordless dialogue with him while still waiting on the day that he will lead us into the house where he has prepared a place for us.

HENRI J. M. NOUWEN,
*REACHING OUT: THE THREE MOVEMENTS
OF THE SPIRITUAL LIFE*

REJOICE!

The Lord is near. Do not worry about anything, but in every-thing by prayer and supplication with thanksgiving let your requests be made known to God. And the peace of God, which surpasses all understanding, will guard your hearts and minds.

PHILIPPIANS 4:5–7

PRAYER

Lord, stretch out our perspective so that it expands in your direction. Remind us that we are not alone and that you are with us. Today we ask you to extend your loving concern to the whole of your earthly peoples, especially to those who have had no chance to know you and your Word directly. Amen.

CHRISTMAS ACTION

In the oft-repeated words of Beatle John Lennon, "Give peace a chance." Today make one effort to restore a modicum of peace in your life.

DAY 4

Turning Loneliness Into Solitude

friend once wrote: "Learning to weep, learning to keep vigil, learning to wait for the dawn. Perhaps this is what it means to be human." It is hard to really believe this because we constantly find ourselves clinging to people, books, events, experiences, projects and plans, secretly hoping that this time it will be different....The few times, however, that we do obey our severe masters and listen carefully to our restless hearts, we may start to sense that in the midst of our sadness there is joy, that in the midst of our fears there is peace, that in the midst of our greediness there is the possibility of compassion.

HENRI J. M. NOUWEN,
*REACHING OUT: THE THREE MOVEMENTS
OF THE SPIRITUAL LIFE*

I WILL EXTOL YOU, O LORD

Sing praises to the LORD,
O you his faithful ones,
and give thanks to his holy name.
For his anger is but for a moment;
his favor is for a lifetime.
Weeping may linger for the night,
but joy comes with the morning....

You have turned my mourning
into dancing;
you have taken off my sackcloth
and clothed me with joy,
so that my soul may praise you
and not be silent.

PSALM 30:4–5, 11–12

PRAYER

Lord, give us the preference and the positive outlook that encourages rejoicing over your arrival among us. Let us surrender all signs of our "sackcloth and weeping" so that we may joyously praise you with song and, yes, even with dancing. Amen.

CHRISTMAS ACTION

Today resolve to practice cheerfulness.

DAY 5

More Than Gifts

*T*rue ministry goes far beyond the giving of gifts. It requires the giving of self. That is the way of him who did not cling to his privileges but emptied himself to share our struggles. When God's way becomes known to us, and practiced by us, hope emerges....

HENRI J. M. NOUWEN,
GRACIAS! A LATIN AMERICAN JOURNAL

Visit of the Wise Men

In the time of King Herod, after Jesus was born in Bethlehem of Judea, wise men from the East came to Jerusalem, asking, "Where is the child who has been born king of the Jews? For we observed his star at its rising, and have come to pay him homage."…When they had heard the king, they set out; and there, ahead of them, went the star that they had seen at its rising, until it stopped over the place where the child was. When they saw that the star had stopped, they were overwhelmed with joy. On entering the house, they saw the child with Mary his mother; and they knelt down and paid him homage. Then, opening their treasure chests, they offered him gifts of gold, frankincense, and myrrh.

MATTHEW 2:1–2, 9–11

Prayer

Lord, as the wise visitors from afar laid their gifts at the feet of the Holy Babe, let us also lay our worries, our defeats, our failures at the manger. Along with these, let us leave our doubts, our hungers, our needs, and our wants so that we may journey unencumbered to the final revelation with you in heaven. Give us, we pray, food and song for the journey. Amen.

Christmas Action

Give gifts symbolizing "gold," "frankincense," and "myrrh" to those who need signs for their journey.

The Wide Embrace, The Narrow Gate

*B*ecoming a child [of God] is living the Beatitudes and so finding the narrow gate into the Kingdom....Isn't the little child poor, gentle, and pure of heart? Isn't the little child weeping in response to every little pain? Isn't the little child the peacemaker hungry and thirsty for uprightness and the final victim of persecution? And what of Jesus himself, the Word of God who became flesh, dwelt for nine months in Mary's womb, and came into this world as a little child worshiped by shepherds from close by and by wise men from far away? The eternal Son became a child so that I might become a child again and so reenter with him into the Kingdom of the Father.

HENRI J. M. NOUWEN,
THE RETURN OF THE PRODIGAL SON:
A STORY OF HOMECOMING

How Great Is the Reward!

Then Jesus looked up at his disciples and said:
"Blessed are you who are poor,
for yours is the kingdom of God.
"Blessed are you who are
hungry now,
for you will be filled.
"Blessed are you who weep now,
for you will laugh.

LUKE 6:20–21

Prayer

Lord, give us beatitude instead of superficial happiness, grant us sorrow for our sins instead of tears over our worldly losses. Lead us to the true food of your bread and wine, body and blood. Amen.

Christmas Action

Today give something away: your place in the grocery checkout line, your custody of the TV remote control, your closed-in parking spot; or do a chore for someone else: walking the dog, loading the dishwasher, or so on.

DAY 7

Only Listen, Only Let Go

E very time I try to meditate on a sacred event such as this [the Presentation at the Temple], I find myself tempted to think about it in an intellectual way. But today I realized more strongly than ever before that I simply have to be there. I have to travel with Mary and Joseph to Jerusalem, walk with them on the busy temple square, join the thousands of simple people in offering their simple gifts,...and listen to two unknown old people who have something to say, something that sounds very strange and even frightening. Why do we want more?...But the story is so simple, so crystal clear, so unpretentious. I do not have to do anything with it. I do not have to explain or examine these events. I simply have to step into them and allow them to surround me.

HENRI J. M. NOUWEN,
GRACIAS! A LATIN AMERICAN JOURNAL

Jesus Is Presented in the Temple

When the time came for their purification according to the law of Moses, they [Joseph and Mary] brought him [the child Jesus] up to Jerusalem to present him to the Lord....

Now there was a man in Jerusalem whose name was Simeon; this man was righteous and devout....It had been revealed to him by the Holy Spirit that he would not see death before he had seen the Lord's Messiah. Guided by the Spirit, Simeon came into the temple; and when the parents brought in the child Jesus, to do for him what was customary under the law, Simeon took him in his arms and praised God, saying,

> *"Master, now you are dismissing*
> *your servant in peace,*
> *according to your word;*
> *for my eyes have seen your*
> *salvation,*
> *which you have prepared in the*
> *presence of all peoples...."*
>
> Luke 2:22, 25–32

Prayer

Lord, prepare us for your presence then, now, and forever. Amen.

Christmas Action

Today resolve to visit an older member of your community or family who is alone. Spend more than a few minutes with him or her. Bring smiles as gifts.

DAY 8

The Discipline of Gratitude

Gratitude as a discipline involves a conscious choice. I can choose to be grateful even when my emotions and feelings are still steeped in hurt and resentment. It is amazing how many occasions present themselves in which I can choose gratitude instead of complaint. I can choose to be grateful when I am criticized, even when my heart responds in bitterness. I can choose to speak about goodness and beauty even when my inner eye still looks for someone to accuse or something to call ugly. I can choose to listen to the voices that forgive and to look at the faces that smile, even while I still hear words of revenge and see grimaces of hatred.

HENRI J. M. NOUWEN,
THE RETURN OF THE PRODIGAL SON:
A STORY OF HOMECOMING

Instructions for a New Life

Let the word of Christ dwell in you richly; teach and admonish one another in all wisdom; and with gratitude in your hearts sing psalms, hymns, and spiritual songs to God. And whatever you do, in word or deed, do everything in the name of the Lord Jesus.

Colossians 3:16–17

Prayer

Lord, as we say and pray your holy name, we declare who you are to us: our savior, our protector, our benefactor who bestows on us eternal life. Intercede with your mother Mary so that this knowledge will be incised forever in our hearts. Amen.

Christmas Action

Be grateful today for all the "little things" done for you that you often may take for granted. Recall this Estonian Proverb: "Who does not thank for little will not thank for much."

DAY 9

Mental Hostility

$\mathcal{F}$ear and hostility are not limited to our encounters with burglars, drug addicts or strangely behaving types. In a world so pervaded with competition, even those who are very close to each other, such as classmates, teammates, colleagues in work, can become infected by fear and hostility when they experience each other as a threat to their intellectual or professional safety. Many places that are created to bring people closer together and help them form a peaceful community have degenerated into mental battlefields. Students in classrooms, teachers in faculty meetings, staff members in hospitals and coworkers in projects often find themselves paralyzed by mutual hostility, unable to realize their purposes because of fear, suspicion, and even blatant aggression.

HENRI J. M. NOUWEN, *REACHING OUT:*
THE THREE MOVEMENTS OF THE SPIRITUAL LIFE

The Example of Jesus

Let us also lay aside every weight and the sin that clings so closely, and let us run with perseverance the race that is set before us, looking to Jesus the pioneer and perfecter of our faith, who for the sake of the joy that was set before him endured the cross, disregarding its shame, and has taken his seat at the right hand of the throne of God. Consider him who endured such hostility against himself from sinners, so that you may not grow weary or lose heart.

HEBREWS 12:1–3

Prayer

Lord, we look to you as the pioneer and perfecter of our faith. Teach us to follow your example in disregarding the arrows of misfortune and enduring the undeserved hostilities also aimed at us. We know that no suffering of ours can remotely equal the ignominy of death on the cross. Amen.

Christmas Action

Take responsibility today for one action that you would rather not claim.

DAY 10

The Discipline of Generosity

*I*n order to become like the Father, I must be as generous as the Father is generous....Every time I take a step in the direction of generosity, I know that I am moving from fear to love. But these steps, certainly at first, are hard to take because there are so many emotions and feelings that hold me back from freely giving. Why should I give energy, time, money, and yes, even attention to someone who has offended me?...

Still...the truth is that, in a spiritual sense, the one who has offended me belongs to my "kin," my "gen." The word "generosity" includes the term "gen" which we also find in the words "gender," "generation," and "generativity." This term, from the Latin *genus* and the Greek *genos*, refers to our being of one kind. Generosity is a giving that comes from the knowledge of that intimate bond. True generosity is acting on the truth—not the feeling—that those I am asked to forgive are "kinfolk," and belong to my family.

HENRI J. M. NOUWEN, *THE RETURN OF THE PRODIGAL SON*

THE GOODNESS OF THE RIGHTEOUS

Be still before the LORD, and wait
*   patiently for him;*
* do not fret over those who*
*   prosper in their way,*
* over those who carry out evil devices.*
Refrain from anger, and forsake wrath.
* Do not fret—it leads only to evil.*
For the wicked shall be cut off,
* but those who wait for the LORD*
*   shall inherit the land....*
Better is a little that the
*   righteous person has*
* than the abundance of many wicked....*
The wicked borrow,
*   and do not pay back,*
* but the righteous are generous*
*   and keep giving.*
            PSALM 37:7–9, 16, 21

PRAYER

Lord, you who were given to the world by your Father, whose gift is beyond all generosity, teach us to give generously out of the love you have granted to us. Amen.

CHRISTMAS ACTION

For today, even though it occurs in the midst of a bleak winter, accept the challenges of life without moaning and groaning about them. After all, these "moans and groans" are really signs of self-centeredness.

DAY 11

Small Gifts, Big Consequences

The world likes things to be large, big, impressive, and elaborate. God chooses the small things which are overlooked in the big world. Andrew's remark, "five barley loaves and two fish; but what is that among so many?" captures well the mentality of a calculating mind. It sounds as if he says to Jesus, "Can't you count? Five loaves and two fish are simply not enough." But for Jesus they were enough….Jesus distributed the loaves and the fish "as much as they wanted."…There is enough, plenty even, for everyone—there are even many leftovers. Here a great mystery becomes visible. What little we give away multiplies. This is the way of God. This is also the way we are called to live our lives. The little love we have, the little knowledge we have, the little advice we have, the little possessions we have, are given to us as gifts of God to be given away. The more we give them away, the more we discover how much there is to give away.

HENRI J. M. NOUWEN, *THE ROAD TO DAYBREAK*

FEEDING THE MULTITUDES

*One of [Jesus'] disciples, Andrew, Simon Peter's brother,
said to him, "There is a boy here who has five barley loaves
and two fish. But what are they among so many people?"
Jesus said, "Make the people sit down." Now there was a
great deal of grass in the place; so they sat down, about five
thousand in all. Then Jesus took the loaves, and when he
had given thanks, he distributed them to those who were
seated; so also the fish, as much as they wanted.*

JOHN 6:8–11

PRAYER

Lord, just as you fed the multitudes with the loaves and
fishes, feed our hungry hearts with the goodness of your
Word. Amen.

CHRISTMAS ACTION

Give the gift of loving attention to others just as Jesus'
solicitude resulted in the multiplication of the loaves and
fish. Notice good will, kind words, overtures to friendship, and so on.

DAY 12

The Water of Purity

*T*oday is the feast of the Baptism of Jesus, a dark and rainy
day. At the [Lourdes] grotto, everything speaks of water:
the rushing Gave River, the drizzling rain from the cloudy sky....

I want to be purified....I go to the baths. There, two men instruct me to undress. They wrap a blue apron around my waist, ask
me to concentrate on what intercessions I want to ask of Mary, then
lead me into the bath and immerse me in the ice-cold water. When
I stand again, they pray the Hail Mary and give me a cup of water
from the spring....Still shivering and wet, I put my clothes back on,
go back to the grotto and pray. Looking up at the statue, I read the
words: "I am the Immaculate Conception," and I understand. The
people of Israel were led through the Red Sea; Jesus was baptized
in the Jordan; someone poured water over my head shortly after I
was born. Blessed are the pure of heart; they shall see God.

HENRI J. M. NOUWEN,
JESUS & MARY: FINDING OUR SACRED CENTER

THE BAPTISM OF JESUS

In those days Jesus came from Nazareth of Galilee and was baptized by John in the Jordan. And just as he was coming up out of the water, he saw the heavens torn apart and the Spirit descending like a dove on him. And a voice came from heaven, "You are my Son, the Beloved; with you I am well pleased."

MARK 1:9–11

PRAYER

Lord, your precursor John the Baptist defended his own ministry yet he cautioned that there was "one among you whom you do not know." Give us, first, the grace to look for you among the crowds and the perseverance to find you even among the commotion. Keep our hearts and our attention fixed on you. Amen.

CHRISTMAS ACTION

Though the baptism of our Lord is not the same kind of baptism that we have received (Christ is, of course, sinless; and we are born with the stain of original sin), use this day to honor your own baptism.

$\mathcal{S}$ources and $\mathcal{P}$ermissions

"I keep expecting loud and impressive events to convince me and others…," p. 2, *Gracias! A Latin American Journal* by Henri J. M. Nouwen, copyright © 1983 by Henri J. M. Nouwen. Reprinted by permission of Harper Collins Publishers, Inc. (paperback published by Orbis, 1993), p. 62.

"The French author Simone Weil writes in her notebook…," page 4, *Out of Solitude: Three Meditations on the Christian Life* by Henri J. M. Nouwen, copyright © 1974, Ave Maria Press, Notre Dame, Indiana. Used with permission of the publisher <www.avemariapress.com>, p. 55.

"Somewhere we know that without a lonely place our lives are in danger…," p. 6, *Out of Solitude: Three Meditations on the Christian Life* by Henri J. M. Nouwen, copyright © 1974, Ave Maria Press, Notre Dame, Indiana. Used with permission of the publisher <www.avemariapress.com>, pp. 14–15.

"Take the gospel of each day and spend ten minutes…," p. 8, Henri J. M. Nouwen interview by Alicia von Stamwitz appearing in *Liguorian* magazine, October 1992. Used by permission.

"If you want to follow Jesus…," p. 10, Henri J. M. Nouwen interview by Alicia von Stamwitz appearing in *Liguorian* magazine, October 1992. Used by permission.

"Jesus didn't live alone. He had Peter, John, and James around…," p. 12, Henri J. M. Nouwen interview by Alicia von Stamwitz appearing in *Liguorian* magazine, October 1992. Used by permission.

"The two main enemies of the spiritual life [are] anger…," p. 14, *The Way of the Heart: Desert Spirituality and Contemporary Ministry* by Henri J. M. Nouwen, copyright © 1981 by Henri J. M. Nouwen. Reprinted by permission of HarperCollins Publishers, Inc., New York, pp. 23–24.

"If you would ask the Desert Fathers why solitude…," p. 16, *The Way of the Heart: Desert Spirituality and Contemporary Ministry* by Henri J. M. Nouwen, copyright © 1981 by Henri J. M. Nouwen. Reprinted by permission of HarperCollins Publishers, Inc., New York, pp. 34–35.

"Mary creates a space for us where we can…," p. 18, *Jesus & Mary: Finding Our Sacred Center* by Henri J. M. Nouwen, St. Anthony Messenger Press: Cincinnati, Ohio, copyright © 1993. Used by permission of the publisher, pp. 13, 16, 17.

"If it is true that God in Jesus Christ is waiting for...," p. 20, Henri J. M. Nouwen, excerpt from the article "The Spirituality of Waiting," *Weavings*, January 1987, The Upper Room, Nashville Tennessee, 1987. Used by permission.

"Keep your eyes on the prince of peace, the one who doesn't...," p. 22, Henri J. M. Nouwen, excerpt from the article "Adam's Story," *Weavings*, March–April 1988, The Upper Room, Nashville, Tennessee, 1988. Used by permission.

"We must continually remind ourselves that the first...," p. 24, *The Living Reminder: Service and Prayer in Memory of Jesus Christ* by Henri J. M. Nouwen, copyright © 1977 by Henri J. M. Nouwen. Reprinted by permission of HarperCollins Publishers, Inc., New York, p. 31.

"The word "listening" in Latin is *obedire*, and *audire*...," p. 26, "Discovering Our Gift Through Service to Others: A Conversation with Henri J. M. Nouwen," transcription of speech given to members of FADICA, 1994. Used by permission.

"I am deeply moved by the simple and mysterious encounter...," p. 28, *The Road to Daybreak: A Spiritual Journey* by Henri J. M. Nouwen, copyright © 1988 by Henri J. M. Nouwen. Used by permission of Doubleday, a division of Random House, Inc., pp. 100–101.

"It is Advent again. In his sermon this morning...," p. 30, *Gracias! A Latin American Journal* by Henri J. M. Nouwen, copyright © 1983 by Henri J. M. Nouwen. Reprinted by permission of HarperCollins Publishers, Inc., New York (paperback published by Orbis, 1993), p. 57.

"The Father's love was so unlimited that he wanted us...," p. 32, *Heart Speaks to Heart: Three Prayers to Jesus* by Henri J. M. Nouwen, copyright © 1989, Ave Maria Press, Notre Dame, Indiana. Used with permission <www.avemariapress.com>, p. 21–22.

"At issue here is the question: "To whom do I...," p. 34, *The Return of the Prodigal Son: The Story of Homecoming* by Henri J. M. Nouwen, copyright © 1992 by Henri J. M. Nouwen. Used by permission of Double-day, a division of Random House, Inc., p. 42.

"One of the greatest ironies of the history of...," p. 36, *In the Name of Jesus: Reflections on Christian Leadership* by Henri J. M. Nouwen, copyright © 1989 by Henri J. M. Nouwen. Reprinted by permission of Crossroad Publishing Company, pp. 58–59.

"Père Thomas keeps telling us in his sermons that the...," p. 38, *The Road to Daybreak: A Spiritual Journey* by Henri J. M. Nouwen, copyright © 1988 by Henri J. M. Nouwen. Used by permission of Doubleday, a division of Random House, Inc., p. 103.

"Jesus' whole message is to say that you are God's…," p. 40, "Discovering Our Gift Through Service to Others: A Conversation with Henri J. M. Nouwen," transcription of speech given to members of FADICA, 1994. Used by permission.

"Quite often out of an intimate encounter with God…," p. 42, "Discovering Our Gift Through Service to Others: A Conversation with Henri J. M. Nouwen," transcription of speech given to members of FADICA, 1994. Used by permission.

"Parker Palmer, a spiritual writer of the Quaker…," p. 44, "Discovering Our Gift Through Service to Others: A Conversation with Henri J. M. Nouwen," transcription of speech given to members of FADICA, 1994. Used by permission.

"In forgiving we are still in control…," p. 46, "Discovering Our Gift Through Service to Others: A Conversation with Henri J. M. Nouwen," transcription of speech given to members of FADICA, 1994. Used by permission.

"God came to us because he wanted to join us on the road…," p. 48, *Gracias! A Latin American Journal* by Henri J. M. Nouwen, copyright © Henri J. M. Nouwen 1983. Reprinted by permission of HarperCollins Publishers, Inc., New York (paperback published by Orbis,1993), p. 82.

"Somehow I realized that songs, music, good feelings…," p. 50, *The Road to Daybreak: A Spiritual Journey* by Henri J. M. Nouwen, copyright © 1988 by Henri J. M. Nouwen. Used by permission of Doubleday, a division of Random House, Inc., pp. 104–105.

"Mysticism is for all, not just for a few special…," p. 52, Henri J. M. Nouwen interview by Alicia von Stamwitz appearing in *Liguorian* magazine, October 1992. Used by permission.

"I know that I am called to live at the place…," p. 54, *Jesus & Mary: Finding Our Sacred Center* by Henri J. M. Nouwen, St. Anthony Messenger Press: Cincinnati, Ohio, 1993. Used by permission of the publisher, pp. 56–57.

"The joyful celebration [of Midnight Mass] unfolded with…," p. 56, *Gracias! A Latin American Journal* by Henri J. M. Nouwen, copyright 1983 by Henri J. M. Nouwen. Reprinted by permission of HarperCollins Publishers, Inc., 1983 (paperback published by Orbis, 1983), pp. 83–84.

"The conviction that Francis Avenue, on which…," p. 60, *The Road to Daybreak: A Spiritual Journey* by Henri J. M. Nouwen, copyright © by Henri J. M. Nouwen 1988. Reprinted by permission of Doubleday, a division of Random House, Inc., p. 9.

"There is a much more human option…," p. 62, *A Letter of Consolation* by Henri J. M. Nouwen, copyright © 1982 by Henri J. M. Nouwen. Reprinted by permission of HarperCollins Publishers, Inc., pp. 51–52.

Scripture Sources Cited

1 John 3:1–2
1 Thessalonians 5:12–18
1 Peter 1:22–23
1 Peter 2:2–3
2 Peter 1:3–4
Colossians 3:12–15
Colossians 3:16–17
Deuteronomy 30:15–18
Ephesians 4:1–6
Hebrews 6:9–12
Hebrews 12:1–3
Isaiah 11:1–3
Isaiah 49:1–2
Isaiah 25:6, 8–9
Jeremiah 1:4–5
John 6:8–11
John 21:18
John 17:15–17
Luke 6:20–21
Luke 2:22, 25–32
Luke 17:3–4

Luke 21:15–18
Luke 1:39–41, 56
Luke 2:1–7
Luke 6:37–38
Luke 12:32–33
Mark 1:9–11
Mark 9:33–35
Mark 1:35–39
Mark 13:32–36
Matthew 11:28–30
Matthew 22:34–38
Matthew 6:25, 32–33
Matthew 2:1–2, 9–11
Matthew 10:1–4
Philippians 4:5–7
Philippians 2:4–8
Psalm 37:7–9, 16, 21
Psalm 23:1–4, 6
Psalm 30:4–5, 11–12
Romans 12:1–2

CPSIA information can be obtained at www.ICGtesting.com
Printed in the USA
LVOW12s2023311014

411430LV00006B/6/P